[redacted]
D1031432

MATH CODES FOR MINECRAFTERS

SKILL-BUILDING PUZZLES AND GAMES FOR HOURS OF ENTERTAINMENT!

JEN FUNK WEBER

NORTHERN PLAINS
PUBLIC LIBRARY
Ault, Colorado

SKY PONY PRESS

This book is not authorized or sponsored by Microsoft Corp., Mojang AB, Notch Development AB or Scholastic Inc., or any other person or entity owning or controlling rights in the Minecraft name, trademark, or copyrights.

Copyright © 2020 by Hollan Publishing, Inc.

Minecraft® is a registered trademark of Notch Development AB.

The Minecraft game is copyright © Mojang AB.

All rights reserved. No part of this book may be reproduced in any manner without the express written consent of the publisher, except in the case of brief excerpts in critical reviews or articles. All inquiries should be addressed to Sky Pony Press, 307 West 36th Street, 11th Floor, New York, NY 10018.

Sky Pony Press books may be purchased in bulk at special discounts for sales promotion, corporate gifts, fund-raising, or educational purposes. Special editions can also be created to specifications. For details, contact the Special Sales Department, Sky Pony Press, 307 West 36th Street, 11th Floor, New York, NY 10018 or info@skyhorsepublishing.com.

Sky Pony® is a registered trademark of Skyhorse Publishing, Inc.®, a Delaware corporation.

Visit our website at www.skyponypress.com.

10 9 8 7 6 5 4 3 2 1

Library of Congress Cataloging-in-Publication Data is available on file.

Cover design by Brian Peterson

Cover and interior illustrations by Amanda Brack

Book design by Kevin Baier

Math codes created by Jen Funk Weber

Print ISBN: 978-1-5107-4724-1

Printed in China

MATH CODES FOR MINECRAFTERS

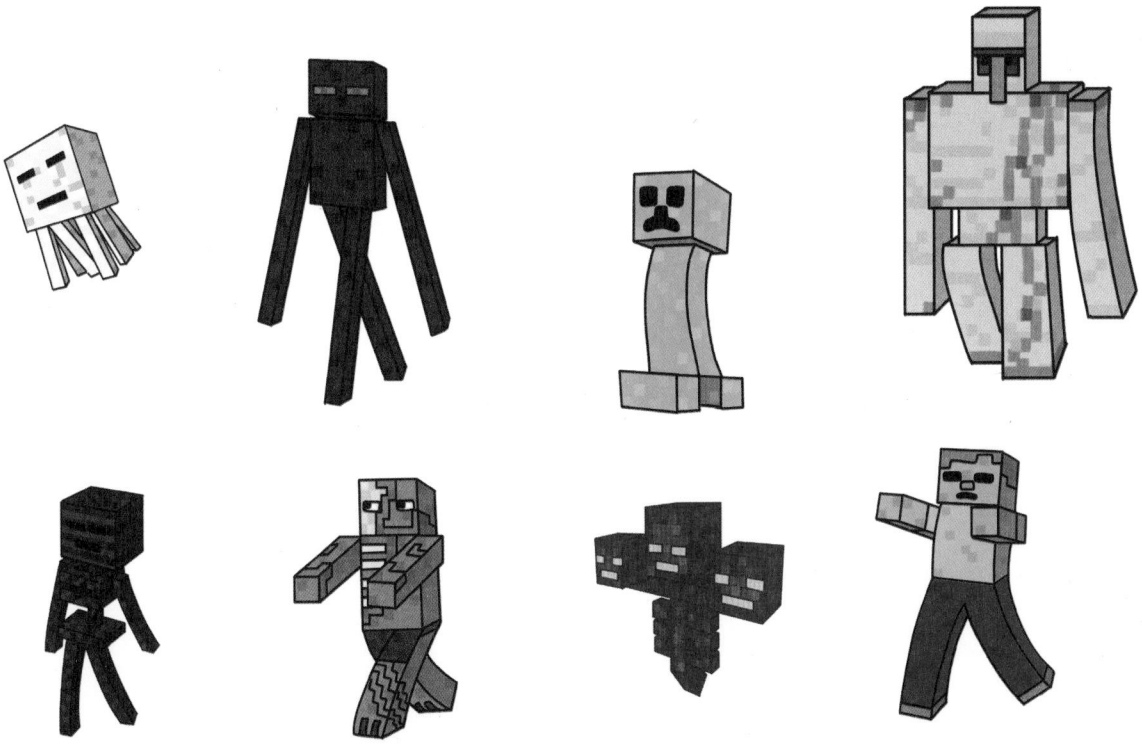

TABLE OF CONTENTS

A Prickly Subject 4
In the Balance 5
Hilarious Haunt 6
Magic Number I 7
A Smashing Success 8
Truth Be Told 9
Treat Yourself to This Trick 10
Don't Let It Roll 11
Fire Away 12
Magic Number II 13
Here, Boy 14
"We Are Number 2, Hey!" 15
Steve Says 16
Endless Enchantments 17
Fire Power 18
Magic Number III 19
Spuh-*lash!* 20
Hunt and Find 21
Inside Riddle 22
Under Pressure 23
Jump Five 24
Magic Number IV 25
Slow Going 26
A Spilled Secret 27
ALERT! ALERT! ALERT! 28
A Balanced Diet 29
Twinzies 30
Magic Number V 31
Looking Up 32
Get Some Perspective 33
What Is the Meaning of This? 34
Payment Balance 35
Magic Number VI 36

Pro Builder Tip 37
Hidden Resource 38
*Neigh*m Your Horse 39
The Point Is . . . Sharp! 40
Ask and Receive 41
Magic Number VII 42
Zombie-Proof 43
A Minecraft Challenge 44
Hidden Passage 45
Your Fate, in the Balance 46
A Nether Joke 47
Magic Number VIII 48
Aim High 49
Minecraft Lingo 50
A Different POV 51
A Sliming Scale 52
Mining Shortcut 53
Fall Fix 54
Balance of Nature 55
Magic Number IX 56
Answers 57

A PRICKLY SUBJECT

Find the sums of the math problems, then use the code-breaker key to reveal the answer to the joke.

24	25	26	27	28	29	30	31	32	33	34	35	36	37	38
A	B	C	D	E	F	G	H	I	J	K	L	M	N	O

39	40	41	42	43	44	45	46	47	48	49
P	Q	R	S	T	U	V	W	X	Y	Z

What would you get if you could breed a pig with a cactus in the Desert biome?

16 + 8 = 24	27 + 12 = ☐	13 + 25 = ☐	34 + 7 = ☐	25 + 9 = ☐	22 + 26 = ☐
	17 + 25 = ☐	14 + 25 = ☐	24 + 8 = ☐	26 + 11 = ☐	19 + 9 = ☐

A ___ ___ ___ ___ ___ ___ ___ ___ ___ ___ ___

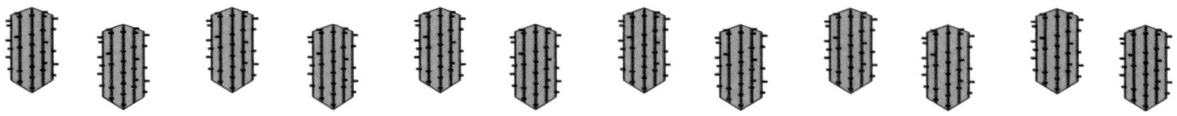

IN THE BALANCE

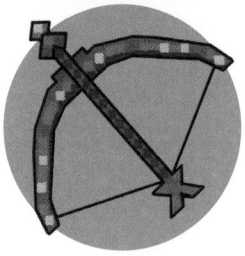

Time to rack up some experience!

The first scale is balanced. You must balance the second scale before it tips, lands on the pressure plate, and launches a hidden arrow right at you!

How many do you need to balance the second scale? Draw them or write the number on the scale.

HILARIOUS HAUNT

Move from box to box as you count by fours. Write the letter from each box where you land on the spaces, in order from left to right. Begin with the number 4 and continue until all the spaces are filled. If you count, hop, and copy letters correctly, you'll reveal the answer to this question:

What might you call a tamed wolf that comes back from the dead?

14 A 24	16 B 44	36 E 20
22 O 8	28 G 34	4 Z 10
18 M 12	26 R 30	40 L 32

Z _____ _____ _____ _____ _____ _____ _____ _____

MAGIC NUMBER 1

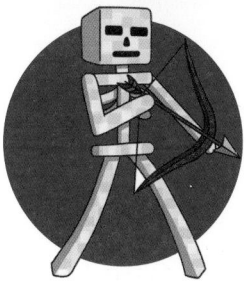

The numbers at the end of the rows are linked to the images in the grid. What number goes in the circle? This is the magic number for this puzzle.

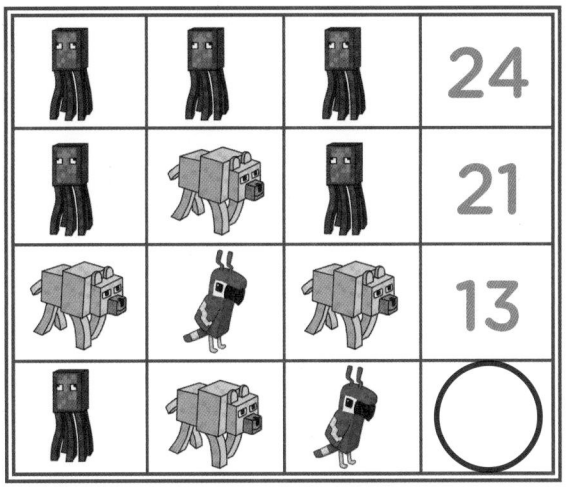

Circle the problems below that have the magic number as their answer. Unscramble those letters to spell the name of a Minecraft mob.

14 +7	17 −6	4 ×4	7 +9	34 −18
A	T	H	O	L
8 ×2	27 −11	4 ×1	12 +4	25 − 9
N	D	R	P	I

___ ___ ___ ___ ___ ___ ___

A SMASHING SUCCESS

Use the picture-number combination under each blank space to find the correct letter on the grid. The correct letter is the one where the picture and number intersect. If you fill in the spaces correctly, you'll discover a fun tip that can help you be a smashing success!

1	T	K	N	A
2	I	U	H	B
3	G	E	R	M
4	C	W	L	O

A player in a minecart on a rail can ride

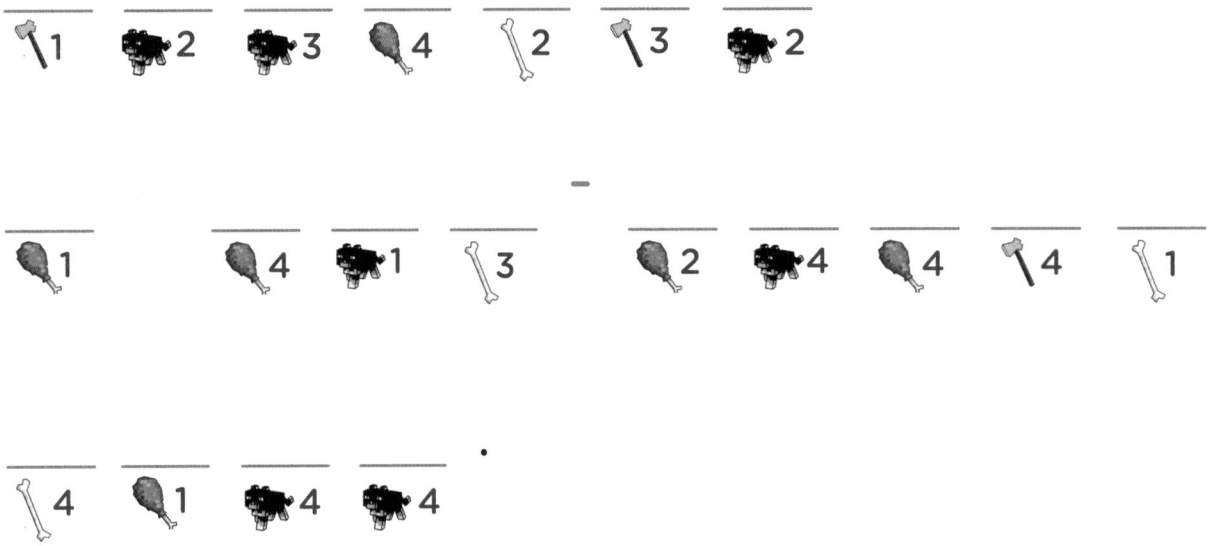

TRUTH BE TOLD

Solve this puzzle and unlock a secret before you're attacked by phantoms! Color every box that has an odd number in it to reveal the word that goes in the blank.

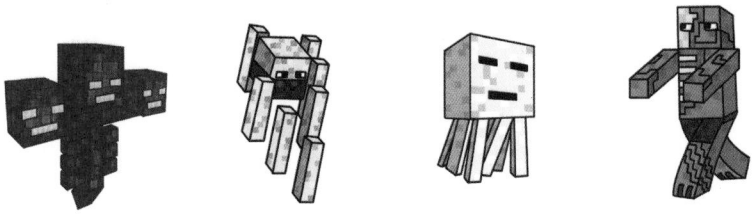

Phantoms were going to be _____,

but designers thought they looked like

Nether mobs.

23	35	18	4	7	39	21	32	13	15	26
17	46	11	28	45	40	12	44	35	48	1
5	43	36	20	29	37	50	2	9	14	21
31	24	27	8	41	16	30	22	35	42	37
49	10	25	38	3	33	47	34	29	45	6

NORTHERN PLAINS
PUBLIC LIBRARY
Ault, Colorado

TREAT YOURSELF TO THIS TRICK

Solve the math problems, then use the code-breaker key to treat yourself to a trick you can play on your Minecrafting friends.

32	33	34	35	36	37	38	39	40	41	42	43	44	45	46
A	B	C	D	E	F	G	H	I	J	K	L	M	N	O

47	48	49	50	51	52	53	54	55	56	57
P	Q	R	S	T	U	V	W	X	Y	Z

Do this with ice blocks, slime, or soul sand:

63 − 24 = ☐

53 − 13 = ☐

99 − 64 = ☐

88 − 52 = ☐

69 − 29 = ☐

89 − 38 = ☐

81 − 29 = ☐

62 − 17 = ☐

76 − 41 = ☐

63 − 27 = ☐

91 − 42 = ☐

92 − 58 = ☐

78 − 46 = ☐

65 − 16 = ☐

54 − 7 = ☐

47 − 11 = ☐

90 − 39 = ☐

___ ___ ___ ___ ___ ___

___ ___ ___ ___ ___ ___ ___ ___ ___ ___ ___

DON'T LET IT ROLL

The first scale is balanced. The second scale is not, and those spawn eggs are about to roll and start a dangerous chain reaction! How many do you need to balance the second scale? Draw them or write the number on the scale.

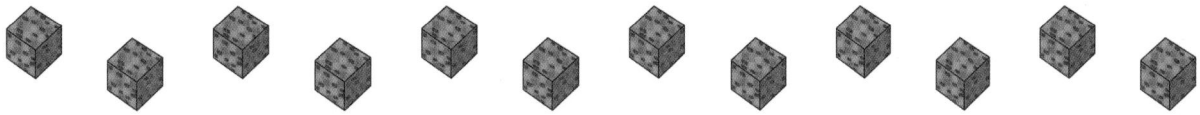

FIRE AWAY

Campfires are useful. Do you know why?

Move from box to box as you count by sixes. Write the letter from each box where you land on the spaces, in order from left to right. Begin with the number 6 and continue until all the spaces are filled. If you count, hop, and copy letters correctly, you'll reveal the one cool thing you can make with a campfire.

27 L 66	52 O 18	36 S 6
48 G 34	42 I 16	10 N 54
12 M 37	30 E 14	68 K 24
60 A 20	26 R 8	11 D 53

S _ _ _ _ _ _ _ _ _ _ _ _

MAGIC NUMBER II

Have you ever seen this mob spawn naturally?

The numbers at the end of the rows and columns are linked to the images in the grid. What number goes in the circle? This is the magic number for this puzzle.

			20
			24
			◯
29	18	25	

Circle problems below that have the magic number as their answer. Unscramble those letters to spell the name of the Minecraft mob that has a very rare 0.164% chance of spawning naturally.

37 − 9	2 × 14	22 + 14	16 + 12	21 + 7	84 ÷ 3
I	E	O	H	E	N
41 − 13	35 − 7	56 ÷ 3	17 + 11	4 × 7	
S	P	N	K	P	

___ ___ ___ ___ ___ ___ ___ ___ ___

HERE, BOY

Use the picture-number combination under each missing letter space to find the correct letter on the grid. The correct letter is the one where the picture and number intersect. If you fill in the spaces correctly, you'll discover the answer to the riddle.

Why are illusioners like well-trained dogs?

1	G	P	A	S
2	O	F	H	C
3	D	I	E	Z
4	L	M	N	R

They come on

"WE ARE NUMBER 2, HEY!"

Hidden in the grid is a mixed-up mob. It's cheering about being #2. Color every box that has an even number in it, then unscramble the letters to reveal a second-place mob and write it on the line.

74	16	32	49	2	43	98	69	43	80	67	89	28	76	10	58	65	96	38	62
59	4	85	97	90	25	6	37	74	77	26	17	50	51	33	81	9	44	91	19
39	28	73	39	34	16	22	77	62	26	18	99	32	47	6	88	67	6	18	52
75	86	7	55	68	27	38	63	8	93	30	45	16	55	79	74	29	23	11	68
41	54	57	95	72	3	56	25	86	61	44	83	66	84	38	22	35	24	76	94

Unscrambled letters:

____ ____ ____ ____ ____

Do you know in what way this mob comes in second?

_____

STEVE SAYS

Steve has a Minecraft saying that he thinks is super clever. Solve the math problems, then use the code-breaker key to complete Steve's favorite saying.

21	22	23	24	25	26	27	28	29	30	31	32	33	34	35
A	B	C	D	E	F	G	H	I	J	K	L	M	N	O

36	37	38	39	40	41	42	43	44	45	46
P	Q	R	S	T	U	V	W	X	Y	Z

Steve's favorite saying:

3 × 9	5 × 5	5 × 7	8 × 4	7 × 5	1 × 27	15 × 3
27						
G	___	___	___	___	___	___

rocks, but

3 × 9	25 × 1	7 × 5	27 × 1	19 × 2	3 × 7	6 × 6	4 × 7	9 × 5
___	___	___	___	___	___	___	___	___

is where it's at!

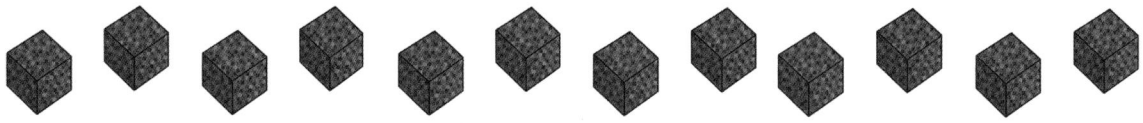

ENDLESS ENCHANTMENTS

The first and second scales are balanced. How many do you need to balance the third scale? Draw them or write the number on the scale. If you balance the scale correctly, you will be able to enchant every item in your inventory!

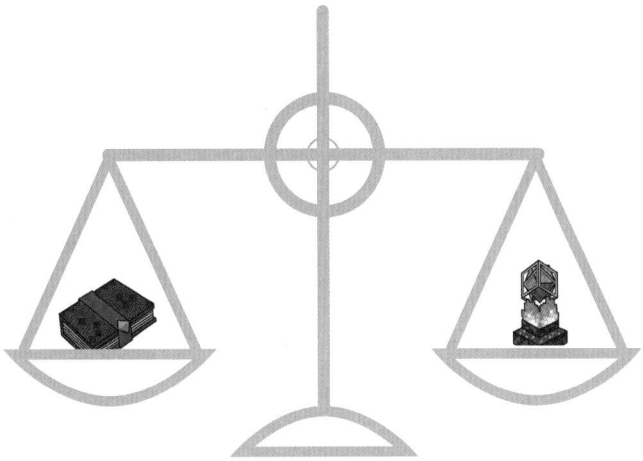

FIRE POWER

Move from box to box as you count by threes. Write the letter from each box where you land on the spaces, in order from left to right. Begin with the number 3 and continue until all the spaces are filled. If you count, hop, and copy letters correctly, you'll fill in the blank below.

A crossbow loaded with fireworks will

damage _____, even at long range.

30 M 18	15 R 25	21 E 19
23 U 13	12 E 3	6 N 24
28 C 16	9 D 27	8 P 22

E _____ _____ _____ _____ _____ _____ _____ _____

MAGIC NUMBER III

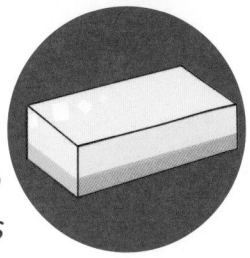

If you fail to solve this puzzle, your ship is sunk!

The numbers at the end of the rows and columns are linked to the images in the grid. What number goes in the circle? This is the magic number for this puzzle.

			41
			31
			27
33	◯	31	

Circle the problems below that have the magic number as their answer. Unscramble those letters to spell the answer to the joke.

Why did the Nitwit sink the boat with too much iron, gold, and redstone?

19 + 16	5 × 7	4 × 8	47 − 12	57 − 22	49 − 7
E	N	J	O	S	G
28 + 7	32 + 3	41 − 6	6 × 2	7 × 5	21 + 14
D	A	E	K	I	R

Because he heard the captain say,

" ___ ___ ___

SPUH-LASH

Splash texts are the yellow lines of text on the title screen. They might be inside jokes, bits of advice, or nonsense.

Use the picture-number combination under each missing letter space to find the correct letter on the grid. The correct letter is the one where the picture and number intersect. If you fill in the spaces correctly, you'll discover splash text that's also a useful piece of Minecraft advice.

1	G	V	E	U
2	A	P	O	D
3	R	I	H	W
4	Z	C	N	T

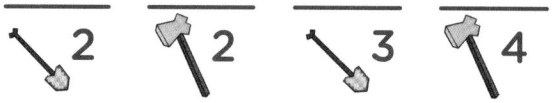

HUNT AND FIND

Color every box that has a multiple of 2 in it to discover what's hidden in the grid. There's loot in it for you, if you can find it.

24	86	12	10	58
68	51	17	25	44
1	70	94	36	73
23	81	35	47	13
26	82	54	18	4
48	95	41	5	33
62	22	34	72	20
9	69	15	21	51
16	40	6	76	94
11	37	19	28	7
31	43	82	61	53
36	50	66	18	70
55	3	45	21	59
2	88	46	72	98
54	25	79	19	26
90	71	94	89	38
38	42	6	83	14
57	93	59	37	53
64	10	78	94	26
54	75	62	29	72
26	39	85	1	34
13	27	65	61	11
74	16	28	50	74
68	39	15	97	92
24	52	60	78	30
87	31	23	99	67
18	34	62	90	58
43	9	55	22	41
17	35	30	57	3
96	68	42	56	74

What? You can't read it? Try turning the page on its side.

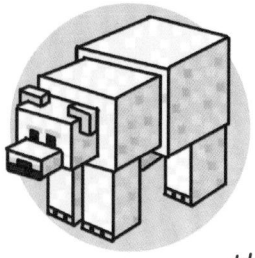

INSIDE RIDDLE

The letters in the code-breaker key spell the answers to both riddles below. Solve the math problems to decipher the answer to the first riddle. Then cross off those letters inside the code-breaker key to reveal the answer to the second riddle.

What large object sometimes generates on a beach?

13	14	15	16	17	18	19	20	21	22	23	24	25	26	27	28
I	S	H	C	I	E	P	W	B	R	E	E	R	C	K	G

12 + 2	31 − 16	6 + 11	27 − 8	5 × 4	17 + 5	6 × 4	34 − 8	9 × 3
14								
S								

Where else does it generate?

___ ___ ___ ___ ___ ___ ___

UNDER PRESSURE

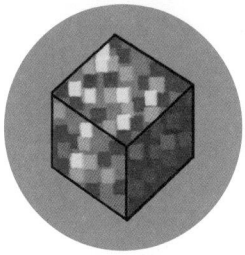

The first and second scales are balanced. How many do you need to balance the third scale? Draw them or write the number on the scale.

If you balance the scale correctly, you'll keep the blocks from rolling off the scale and avoid a dangerous chain reaction.

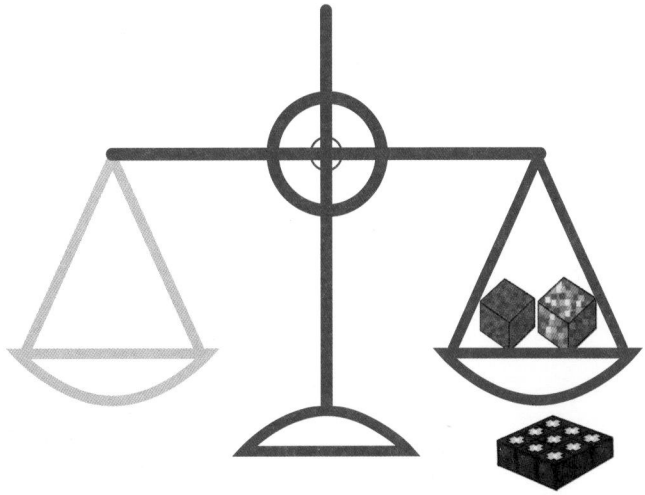

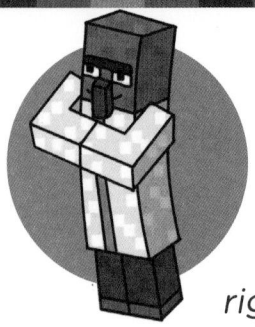

JUMP FIVE

Beginning with the number 19, jump from box to box by adding 5 each time you move. Write the letter from each box where you land on the blank letter spaces, in order from left to right. You'll reveal a Minecraft game where players jump around.

29 R 49	59 N 28	39 O 79
44 U 35	40 E 64	45 A 24
29 P 19	9 K 34	8 L 22

P___ ___ ___ ___ ___ ___ ___

MAGIC NUMBER IV

The numbers at the end of the rows are linked to the images in the grid. What number goes in the circle? This is the magic number.

Circle the problems below that have the magic number as their answer. Unscramble those letters to spell the name of a Minecraft mob.

28 + 2 ___	6 x5 ___	26 + 4 ___	33 - 22 ___	17 +24 ___	15 x 2 ___
N	L	G	I	R	E
21 +9 ___	51 -11 ___	16 +14 ___	76 -46 ___	53 -23 ___	42 -12 ___
W	C	O	M	S	O

___ ___ ___ ___ ___ ___ ___ ___ ___

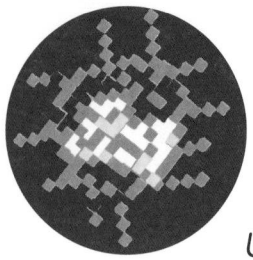

SLOW GOING

Cobwebs are great for slowing down mobs and arrows, but they have another clever use, too.

Use the picture-number combination under each blank letter space to find the correct letter on the grid. The correct letter is the one where the picture and number intersect. If you fill in the spaces correctly, you'll discover another fun use for cobwebs.

Use cobwebs to create delays in _____.

1	D	A	T	N
2	U	B	K	R
3	O	C	S	G
4	W	E	L	I

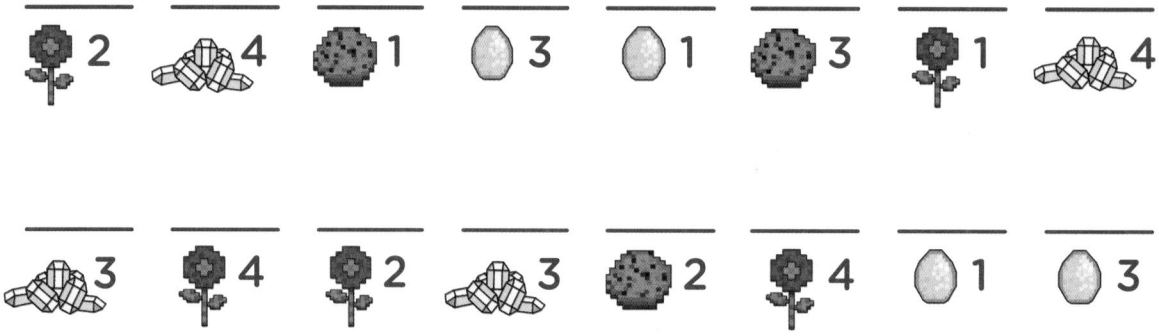

A SPILLED SECRET

It's more of a cure than a secret, really, but you still don't want to spill it.

Color every box that has a multiple of 3 in it to reveal this handy item.

78	84	22	30	18	65	6	16	75	49	69	20	53	99
36	17	60	43	45	70	41	35	90	4	33	64	42	58
57	14	51	65	24	88	42	50	27	31	51	96	56	44
21	2	28	91	33	61	54	11	63	73	45	62	39	27
45	37	19	8	42	7	15	26	48	56	60	7	22	75

ALERT! ALERT! ALERT!

Use this handy trick to stay safe when you're working in your Minecraft house . . . or office . . . or lab . . . or anywhere indoors.

Solve the math problems, then use the code-breaker key to reveal this useful tip.

14	15	16	17	18	19	20	21	22	23	24	25	26	27	28
A	B	C	D	E	F	G	H	I	J	K	L	M	N	O

29	30	31	32	33	34	35	36	37	38	39
P	Q	R	S	T	U	V	W	X	Y	Z

If you want to hear when hostile mobs are approaching, surround your building with

18 + 11	5 x 5	22 - 8	54 ÷ 2	3 x 8	28 + 4
29					
P					

A BALANCED DIET

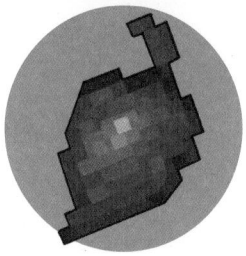

You've gotta eat to survive!

The first and second scales are balanced. How many do you need to balance the third scale? Draw them or write the number on the scale.

If you balance the scale correctly, you will refill your hunger bar.

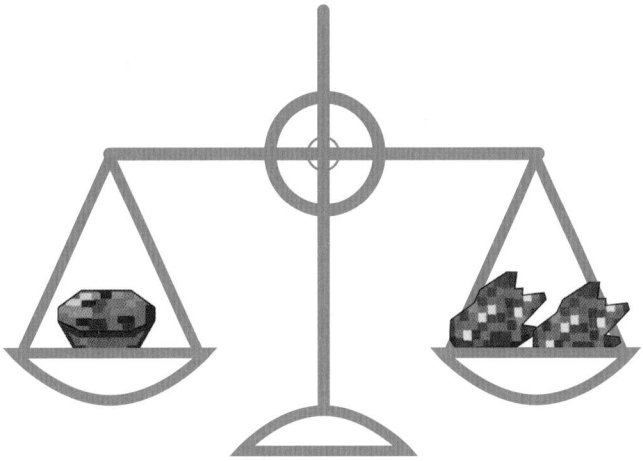

TWINZIES

Beginning with the number 75, count up by fives. Write the letter from each box where you land on the spaces, in order from left to right until all spaces are filled.

If you count, hop, and copy letters correctly, you'll reveal the answer to this question:

What do you call Alex's zombie twin?

84 E 120	115 G 96	93 O 145	100 R 125
130 X 99	82 I 105	75 A 90	111 E 85
101 O 135	95 D 80	106 C 140	79 N 110

A ___ ___ ___ ___

___ ___ ___ ___ ___ ___

MAGIC NUMBER V

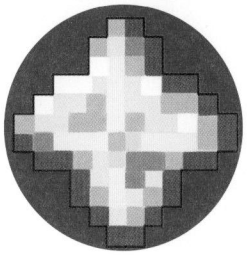

The numbers at the end of the rows are linked to the images in the grid. What number goes in the circle? This is the magic number for this puzzle.

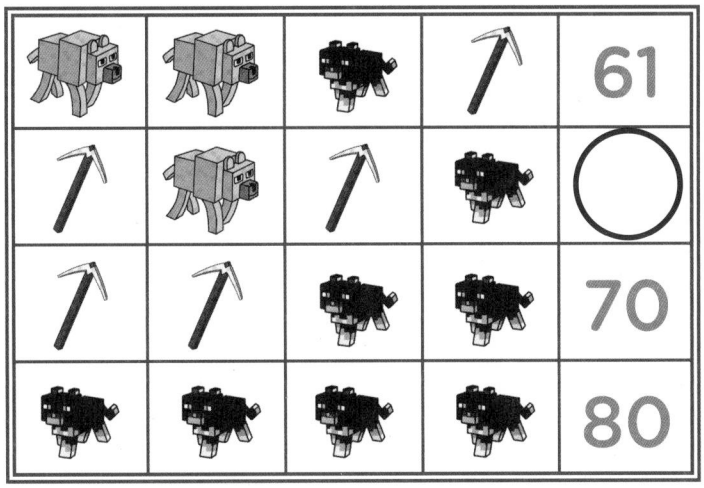

Circle the problems below that have the magic number as their answer. Unscramble those letters to reveal a play mode that gives you more control over the Minecraft world.

76 -13	8 x7	45 + 2	7 x9	91 -28
F	N	A	U	F
98 -34	47 +16	84 -19	21 x 3	28 +35
G	B	B	E	T

___ ___ ___ ___ ___ ___

NORTHERN PLAINS
PUBLIC LIBRARY
Ault, Colorado

LOOKING UP

Have you ever gotten lost in Minecraft? Use the picture-number combination under each blank letter space to find the correct letter on the grid. The correct letter is the one where the picture and number intersect. If you fill in the spaces correctly, you'll discover a unique method for finding your way in Minecraft.

1	O	A	T	H
2	Y	P	E	M
3	B	K	W	R
4	L	V	X	S

Watch the sun, moon, stars, and clouds, because they

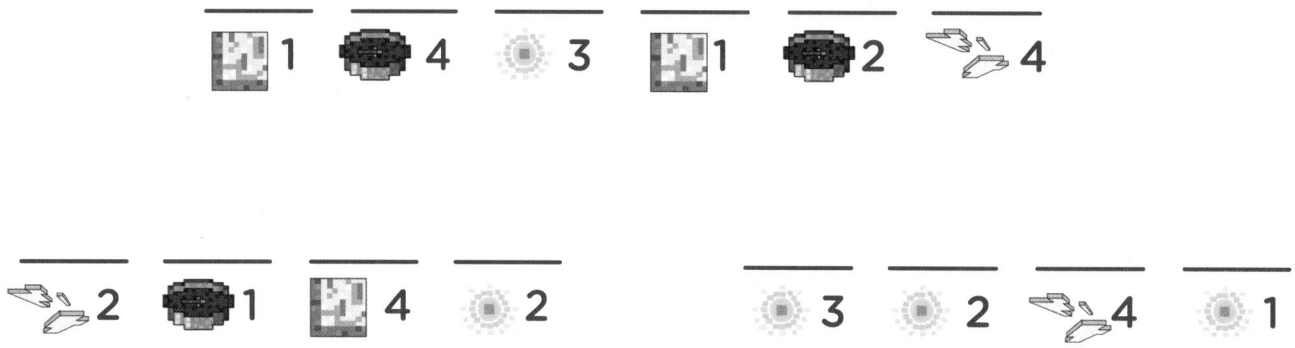

GET SOME PERSPECTIVE

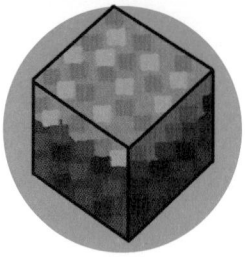

Color every box that has a multiple of 5 to reveal the key on your keyboard that changes your view in the game from first person to third person. Hint: *The answer lies in the uncolored squares.*

What is the key? _____

14	58	22	30	17	63	92
39	75	15	50	87	20	45
66	4	60	25	51	42	6
48	80	5	40	35	10	27
52	65	70	55	11	49	88

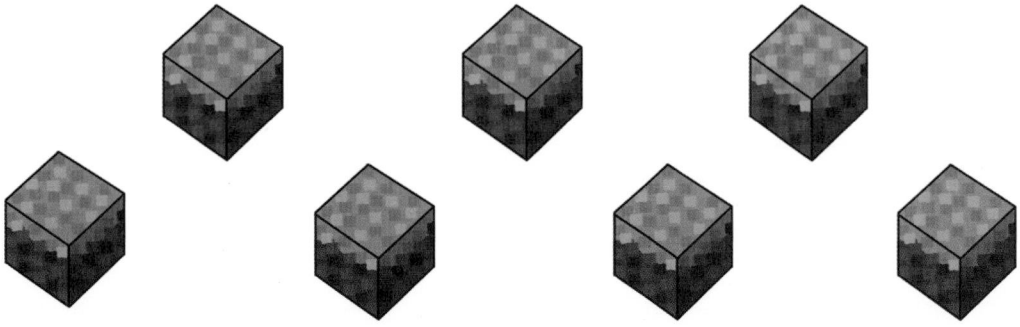

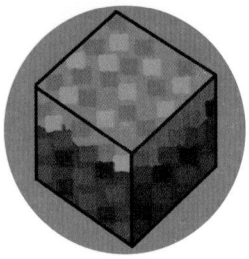

WHAT IS THE MEANING OF THIS?

Solve the math problems, then use the code-breaker key to reveal a fun fact about the company that makes Minecraft.

48	49	50	51	52	53	54	55	56	57	58	59	60	61	62
A	B	C	D	E	F	G	H	I	J	K	L	M	N	O

63	64	65	66	67	68	69	70	71	72	73
P	Q	R	S	T	U	V	W	X	Y	Z

20 x 3	38 +24	19 x 3	96 ÷ 2	98 −37	18 x 3
" 60					"
M					

is a

99 −33	35 x 2	43 + 9	17 x 3	72 −16	38 +28	11 x 5	10 x 7	18 +44	84 −19	93 −42

9 x 6	29 +19	73 −22	48 + 6	71 −19	33 +34
meaning "					. "

PAYMENT BALANCE

Villagers insist you balance the payment scales below. If you don't, they vow to pillage your inventory.

The first and second scales are balanced. How many do you need to balance the third scale? Draw them or write the number on the scale.

MAGIC NUMBER VI

The numbers at the end of the rows and columns are linked to the images in the grid. What number goes in the circle? This is the magic number for this puzzle.

				42
				84
				◯
				47
39	55	64	67	

Circle the problems below that have the magic number as their answer. Unscramble those letters to reveal a clever way to locate hidden caves.

79	13	64	18	8	25
-25	x4	-12	x 3	x6	+27
E	O	S	A	D	P

78	41	13	26	80
-26	+ 2	+39	x 2	+24
I	B	T	N	C

___ ___ ___ ___ ___ ___

PRO BUILDER TIP

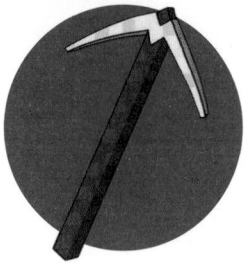

Design and build cool structures and scenes with this pro tip.

Use the picture-number combination under each blank letter space to find the correct letter on the grid. The correct letter is the one where the picture and number intersect. If you fill in the spaces correctly, you'll discover a unique method for crafting amazing buildings and landscapes.

1	I	T	L	R
2	W	E	U	A
3	N	Q	S	H
4	M	G	V	D

Use ____ ____ ____ ____ ____

3 1 4 3 3

and ____ ____ ____ ____ ____ ____ ____

1 2 4 4 2 1 3

to stop ____ ____ ____ ____ ____

2 2 1 2 1

and ____ ____ ____ ____.

1 2 4 2

HIDDEN RESOURCE

Color every box with a number that is divisible by 3. If you color the boxes correctly, you'll shed some light on a useful Minecraft item.

33	15	81	86	75	39	24	70	66	30	72	11	72	3	18	34	75	19	87
8	90	76	35	42	89	51	43	93	91	87	82	36	55	96	74	99	61	57
26	48	41	20	96	14	78	1	6	12	54	2	21	59	79	25	15	60	24
77	63	67	47	36	83	45	88	54	81	32	65	9	17	42	68	51	80	39
49	9	22	40	21	69	18	71	84	94	90	85	48	66	84	46	78	13	45

NEIGHM YOUR HORSE

Is there such a thing as too many Minecraft jokes? Neigh!

Find the sums of the math problems, then use the code-breaker key to decipher the punchline of this joke.

48	49	50	51	52	53	54	55	56	57	58	59	60	61	62
A	B	C	D	E	F	G	H	I	J	K	L	M	N	O

63	64	65	66	67	68	69	70	71	72	73
P	Q	R	S	T	U	V	W	X	Y	Z

Alex calls her horse "Mayo," and

54 + 12	27 + 35	69 − 9	31 + 21	12 + 55	63 − 7	34 + 26	11 + 41	22 x 3
66								
S								

31 + 29	64 − 16	31 + 41	31 x 2	90 − 29	75 − 23	8 x 7	84 − 30	72 − 17	11 x 6

THE POINT IS... SHARP!

The first and second scales are balanced. How many do you need to balance the third scale? Draw them or write the number on the scale before the cactus rolls and you feel its spikes. Ouch!

ASK AND RECEIVE

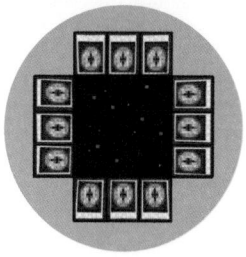

Hop from box to box counting by sevens. Write the letter from each box where you land on the spaces, in order from left to right, until all spaces are filled.

If you count, hop, and copy letters correctly, you'll reveal the decorative item that was added at the suggestion of a Minecraft fan like you.

31 I 7	35 F 46	62 U 45	56 M 28
60 R 42	70 S 25	22 T 14	38 Y 29
50 D 13	24 Q 32	63 E 21	43 A 49

I

___ ___ ___ ___

___ ___ ___ ___ ___ ___

MAGIC NUMBER VII

The numbers at the end of the rows and columns are linked to the images in the grid. What number goes in the circle? This is the magic number for this puzzle.

				43
				53
				42
				53
◯	52	40	51	

Circle the problems below that have the magic number as their answer. Unscramble those letters to spell the name of a Minecraft mob.

6 x 8	17 +31	2 x 24	57 - 9	7 x 7	36 +13
S	I	H	L	A	B
60 -12	12 x 4	33 +15	4 x 12	16 x 3	29 +19
R	S	V	F	E	I

___ ___ ___ ___ ___ ___ ___ ___ ___ ___

ZOMBIE-PROOF

Use the picture-number combination under each space to find the correct letter on the grid. The correct letter is the one where the picture and number intersect. If you fill in the spaces correctly, you'll discover a useful Minecraft tip for protecting yourself from zombies.

1	O	V	C	I
2	B	S	L	D
3	F	G	R	M
4	J	N	A	E

Want to zombie-proof your castle?

make excellent

A MINECRAFT CHALLENGE

Solve this puzzle to reveal a particular kind of Minecraft challenge! Color every box with a number that is divisible by 4.

92	32	60	14	96	12	68	58	8	38	22	54	96
56	34	4	22	78	44	18	70	64	28	10	24	48
24	62	14	30	38	84	42	46	88	72	36	56	52
80	94	48	74	66	52	10	82	40	98	92	26	16
36	72	16	50	18	20	34	26	76	90	86	42	68

HIDDEN PASSAGE

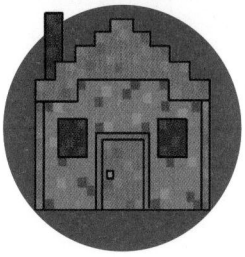

Use your math skills to crack the code. Solve the math problems and use the code-breaker key to find the letters that spell out where you can find a hidden passage.

9	10	11	12	13	14	15	16	17	18
S	E	T	N	R	D	O	P	N	O

19	20	21	22	23	24	25	26	27
G	R	H	T	O	A	L	L	D

3	45	7	24	15	12	3	31	5	19
x 3	-34	+ 6	- 9	+ 2	+ 7	x 7	- 8	x 5	+ 8

Now, cross out the letters you used in the code-breaker key and write the remaining letters in order on the space below.

What is the hidden passage called?

_____

YOUR FATE, IN THE BALANCE

As long as the scales are balanced, you are safe. As soon as one tips, even the slightest bit, you're a goner. The first and second scales are balanced. How many do you need to balance the third scale? Draw them or write the number on the scale before the lava or the husks destroy you!

A NETHER JOKE

Beginning with the number 14, move from box to box by adding 3 each time you move. Write the letter from each box where you land on the spaces, in order from left to right, until all spaces are filled. If you count, hop, and copy letters correctly, you'll reveal the punchline to this joke:

Did you hear about the Minecraft player who went to sleep in the Nether?

20 C 11	50 E 29	23 A 38	53 N 46
35 O 59	14 H 55	22 A 33	32 T 51
26 M 37	47 D 56	17 E 44	8 B 41

H ___ ___ ___ ___ ___ ___ ___ ___

___ ___ ___ ___ ___ ___ ___!

MAGIC NUMBER VIII

The numbers at the end of the rows and columns are linked to the images in the grid. What number goes in the circle? This is the magic number for this puzzle.

				43
				34
				38
				◯
50	33	48	24	

Circle the problems below that have the magic number as their answer. Unscramble those letters to spell the name of a new, underwater block that can be activated to attack hostile mobs.

8	18	26	48	4
x 5	+13	+14	- 8	x 10
D	E	I	U	C
57	2	47	62	27
-17	x20	- 9	x 2	+13
N	T	L	S	O

___ ___ ___ ___ ___ ___ ___

AIM HIGH

Reaching higher altitudes is possible only if you know this trick. Use the picture-number combination under each blank letter space to find the correct letter on the grid. The correct letter is the one where the picture and number intersect. If you fill in the spaces correctly, you'll discover a useful Minecraft skill.

1	L	N	E	J
2	C	U	P	G
3	I	S	T	R
4	O	A	M	K

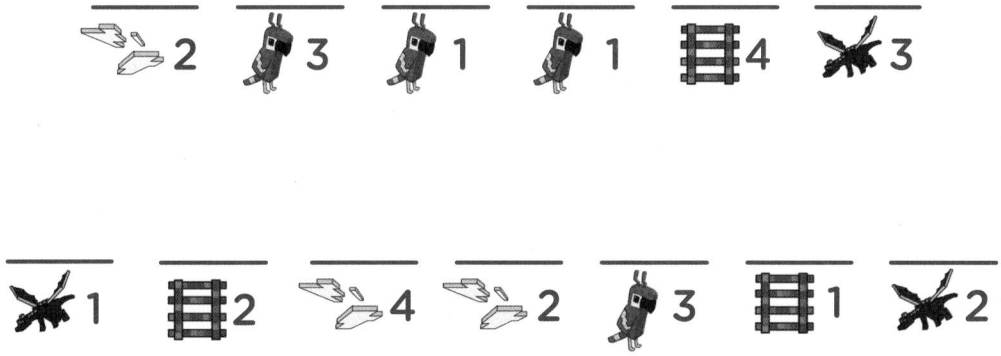

MINECRAFT LINGO

Are you up on Minecraft lingo? Color every box that contains a multiple of 7. If you color the boxes correctly, you'll reveal a term that competitive Minecrafters know.

37	54	77	47	38	84	32	94	60	81	42
64	50	35	92	28	61	14	37	45	34	91
70	14	63	59	56	43	77	65	98	42	56
84	73	7	31	42	72	63	52	35	86	49
98	21	49	87	91	36	14	46	70	28	7

Wait a minute, that's not right! Try turning the book upside down to read the term for competitive gaming.

A DIFFERENT POV

Solve the math problems, then use the code-breaker key to figure out which option in Minecraft allows you to turn everything black and white or upside down.

37	38	39	40	41	42	43	44	45	46	47	48	49	50	51
A	B	C	D	E	F	G	H	I	J	K	L	M	N	O

52	53	54	55	56	57	58	59	60	61	62
P	Q	R	S	T	U	V	W	X	Y	Z

14 + 41	19 x 3	13 x 4	39 + 2	70 − 16
55				
S	___	___	___	___

81 − 26	66 − 25	40 − 1	42 +12	26 +15	14 x 4
___	___	___	___	___	___

37 +18	80 − 39	67 − 11	48 + 8	9 x 5	77 − 27	27 +16	72 − 17
___	___	___	___	___	___	___	___

A SLIMING SCALE

The first and second scales are balanced. How many do you need to balance the third scale? Draw them or write the number on the scale. If you balance the scale correctly, you get to keep the redstone.

MINING SHORTCUT

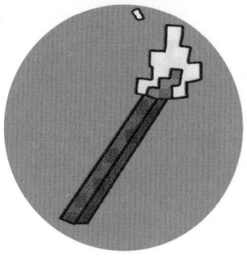

This shortcut can save you tons of time. Beginning with the number 22, move from box to box by adding 4 each time you move. Write the letter from each box where you land on the spaces, in order from left to right, until all spaces are filled. If you count, hop, and copy letters correctly, you'll reveal a time-saving mining technique.

30 N 84	86 S (22)	78 H 56	82 E 54
25 I 72	58 L 32	42 R 70	34 D 40
66 O 90	92 G 38	52 Y 60	88 T 62
50 V 94	80 F 76	46 A 26	74 C 64

Mine S ___ ___ ___ and ___ ___ ___ ___ ___ ___

with ___ ___ ___ ___ ___ ___ ___.

NORTHERN PLAINS
PUBLIC LIBRARY
Ault, Colorado

FALL FIX

Have you ever been destroyed in the game by a bad fall? Next time, use this to survive. Solve the math problems, then use the code-breaker key to reveal a handy tip for avoiding falls.

45	46	47	48	49	50	51	52	53	54	55	56	57	58	59
A	B	C	D	E	F	G	H	I	J	K	L	M	N	O

60	61	62	63	64	65	66	67	68	69	70
P	Q	R	S	T	U	V	W	X	Y	Z

15 × 3	61 − 15	5 × 13	38 + 9	98 − 43	7 × 7	8 × 8
45						
A	___	___	___	___	___	___

32 + 27	10 × 5	91 − 24	43 + 2	16 × 4	82 − 33	27 + 35
___	___	___	___	___	___	___

BALANCE OF NATURE

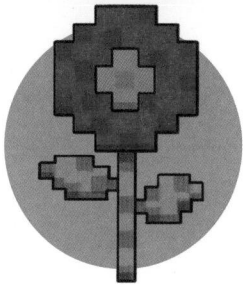

Can you preserve the delicate balance of nature? The first and second scales are balanced. How many do you need to balance the third scale? Draw them or write the number on the scale.

MAGIC NUMBER IX

The numbers at the end of the rows and columns are linked to the images in the grid. What number goes in the circle? This is the magic number for this puzzle.

				26
				◯
				36
				31
27	34	30	31	

Write the magic number on the left-most line below. Subtract 25 from this magic number to find out how many chicks can spawn from one Minecraft chicken egg.

_____ - 25 = _____ chicks

ANSWERS

PAGE 4
A PRICKLY SUBJECT
A PORKYSPINE

PAGE 5
IN THE BALANCE
4 experience orbs

PAGE 6
HILARIOUS HAUNT
ZOMBEAGLE

PAGE 7
MAGIC NUMBER 1
16 - DOLPHIN

PAGE 8
A SMASHING SUCCESS
A player in a minecart on a rail can ride THROUGH A ONE-BLOCK WALL

PAGE 9
TRUTH BE TOLD

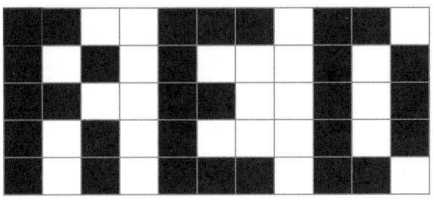

PAGE 10
TREAT YOURSELF TO THIS TRICK
Do this with ice blocks, slime, or soul sand: HIDE IT UNDER CARPET. Friends won't see it, but the effects will still work, so they'll slip, bounce, or slooooooow down.

PAGE 11
DON'T LET IT ROLL
9 zombie pigman spawn eggs

PAGE 12
FIRE AWAY
SMOKE SIGNAL

PAGE 13
MAGIC NUMBER 11
28 - PINK SHEEP

PAGE 14
HERE, BOY
They come on COMMAND.
Get it? Illusioners don't spawn naturally, but you can make them spawn with the /summon illusioner command.

PAGE 15
"WE ARE NUMBER 2, HEY!"

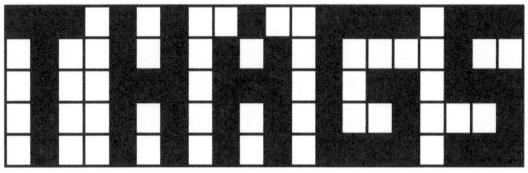

The mob is the GHAST, and it is the second largest mob in Minecraft. The Ender Dragon is largest.

PAGE 16
STEVE SAYS
GEOLOGY rocks, but GEOGRAPHY is where it's at!

PAGE 17
ENDLESS ENCHANTMENTS
4 enchanted books

PAGE 18
FIRE POWER
ENDERMEN

PAGE 19
MAGIC NUMBER III
35 - Because the captain of the ship said, "I NEED OARS!"

PAGE 20
SPUH-*LASH*!
NEVER DIG DOWN

PAGE 21
HUNT AND FIND

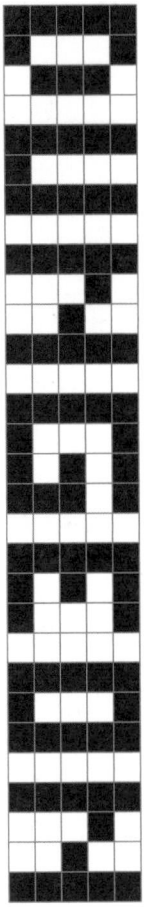

PAGE 22
INSIDE RIDDLE
SHIPWRECK, ICEBERG
In Minecraft, shipwrecks usually generate in oceans and on beaches, but occasionally they will generate in icebergs.

PAGE 23
UNDER PRESSURE
11 sponge blocks

PAGE 24
JUMP FIVE
PARKOUR

PAGE 25
MAGIC NUMBER IV
30 - SNOW GOLEM

PAGE 26
SLOW GOING
Use cobwebs to create delays in REDSTONE CIRCUITS.

PAGE 27
A SPILLED SECRET

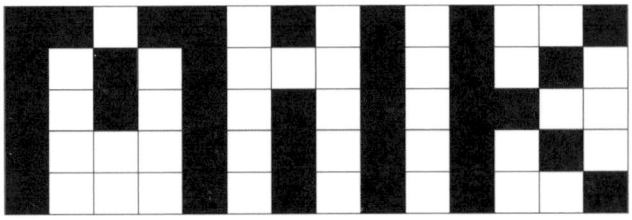

Drinking milk cures negative status effects, but it also wipes out positive ones.

PAGE 28
ALERT! ALERT! ALERT!
Surround your building with PLANKS, then you'll hear mobs when they walk on them.

PAGE 29
A BALANCED DIET
9 beets

PAGE 30
TWINZIES
A DEAD RINGER

PAGE 31
MAGIC NUMBER V

63 - BUFFET
You choose how a Buffet world is customized.

PAGE 32
LOOKING UP

ALWAYS MOVE WEST

PAGE 33
GET SOME PERSPECTIVE

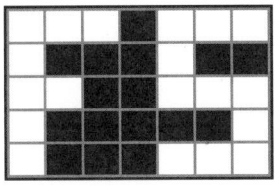

F5 shows up in the negative space of this puzzle. It is a function key on a keyboard, and it's used to change the player's perspective. For instance, you can see the back of your head or even your face as you play the game.

PAGE 34
WHAT IS THE MEANING OF THIS?

"MOJANG" is a SWEDISH WORD meaning "GADGET."
Mojang (pronounced "mo-YANG") is the name of the company that makes Minecraft.

PAGE 35
PAYMENT BALANCE

2 gold ingots

PAGE 36
MAGIC NUMBER VI

52 - PISTON
A piston can be placed against a wall where you think a cave is hiding. If it pushes out, that means there might be a cave within 12 blocks. Dig for it!

PAGE 37
PRO BUILDER TIP

Use SIGNS and LADDERS to stop WATER and LAVA.

PAGE 38
HIDDEN RESOURCE

PAGE 39
***NEIGHM* YOUR HORSE**

Alex calls her horse "Mayo," and SOMETIMES MAYO NEIGHS!

PAGE 40
THE POINT IS . . . SHARP!

12 guardians

PAGE 41
ASK AND RECEIVE

ITEM FRAMES

PAGE 42
MAGIC NUMBER VII

48 - SILVERFISH

PAGE 43
ZOMBIE-PROOF

FENCES make excellent DOORS. Zombies can't break the fences, and you can fight back through the fences. Genius!

PAGE 44
A MINECRAFT CHALLENGE

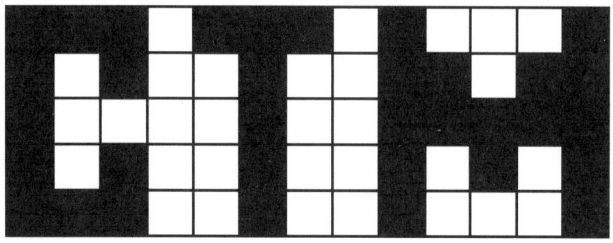

CTM (Complete the Monument.)

PAGE 45
HIDDEN PASSAGE

STRONGHOLD
END PORTAL

PAGE 46
YOUR FATE, IN THE BALANCE

9 creepers

PAGE 47
A NETHER JOKE

Did you hear about the Minecraft player who went to sleep in the Nether? HE CAME TO A BED END.

PAGE 48
MAGIC NUMBER VIII

40 - CONDUIT

PAGE 49
AIM HIGH

PILLAR JUMPING - The pillar is placed while you're jumping.

PAGE 50
MINECRAFT LINGO

PVP stands for Player vs. Player.

PAGE 51
A DIFFERENT POV

SUPER SECRET SETTINGS

PAGE 52
A SLIMING SCALE

12 slime blocks

PAGE 53
MINING SHORTCUT

Mine SAND and GRAVEL with TORCHES.

PAGE 54
FALL FIX

A BUCKET OF WATER

PAGE 55
BALANCE OF NATURE

6 flowers

PAGE 56
MAGIC NUMBER IX

29 - 4 chicks

CERTIFICATE OF ACHIEVEMENT

CONGRATULATIONS

This certifies that

_____

Name

became a

MINECRAFT PUZZLE BOSS

on _____.

Date

_____

Signature

ALSO AVAILABLE

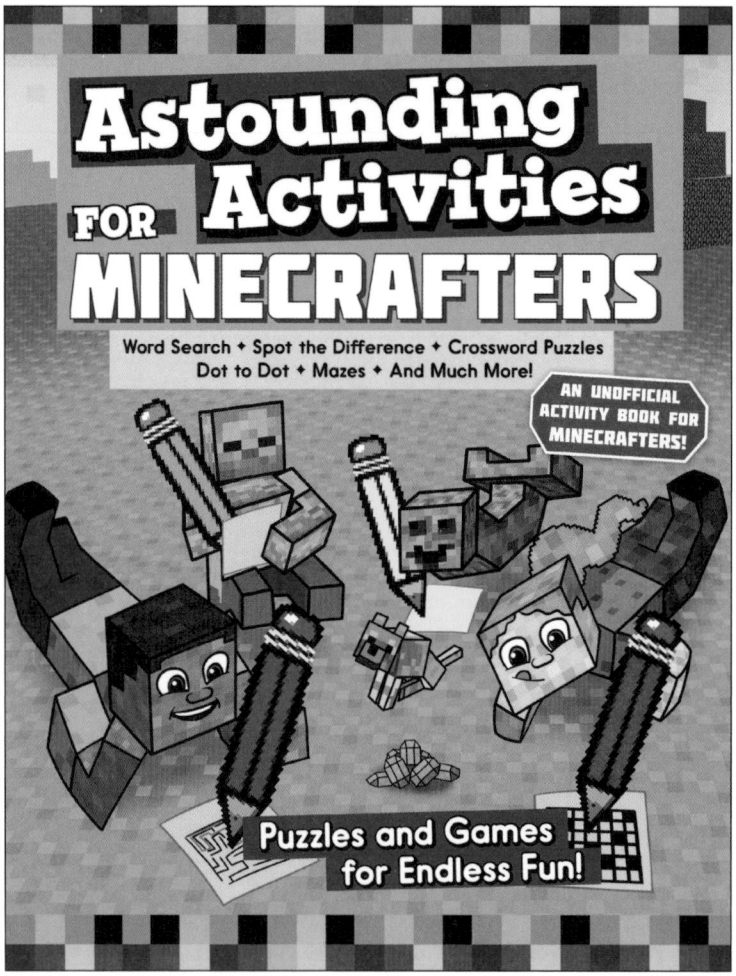